Ladybird

D0501604

BIRDS

CONTENTS

page

What Are Birds?. 5

Seedeaters. 6

Fruit Eaters 8

Tropical Nectar Feeders. 10

Insect Eaters. 12

Fish Eaters 14

Birds of Prey and Scavengers 16

foldout: The Andean Condor . . .18-21

foldout: Built for Flight 22-24

Eggs and Hatching 25

Interesting Bird Behavior 26

Starting a Family 28

Birds on the Move 30

Birds in Danger 32

Saving Birds 34

Amazing Bird Facts. 36

Glossary. 37

Index 38

WHAT ARE BIRDS?

Birds are warm-blooded, egg-laying creatures with two wings, a beak, and scale-covered legs and feet. Unlike any other group of animals, birds are covered with feathers. There are more than 8,700 species of birds.

Archaeopteryx
This is the oldest known bird, which lived 150 million years ago. Most scientists now agree that birds descended from a group of dinosaurs called maniraptors.

Bee Hummingbird
The smallest bird in the world is the Cuban bee hummingbird found in Cuba and the Isle of Pine. It is shown here at full size.

Moa and Ostrich
At over 13 feet high, moas were the tallest birds ever to live on Earth. They lived in New Zealand and were hunted by the Maoris who settled there. Moas became **extinct** in the 1800s. The ostrich lives in Africa and is the largest bird alive today. When fully grown it is taller than an adult person.

SEEDEATERS

Birds that feed mainly on the seeds of different plants are commonly called finches. These birds will also collect insects, which are easier to digest, to feed to their young. Finches are often small, and sometimes live together in **flocks**.

Tough Seeds

The finch's short, stout beak helps it break open a seed's hard covering to reach the kernel inside.

Beak of a Seedeater

Powerful bill

Sharp edge for crushing

Woodpecker Finch

This finch, found in the Galapagos Islands, is one of the few animals that has learned to use a tool. It breaks off cactus spines and uses them to poke under the bark of trees to find insects.

Darwin's Finches

In the 1800s, Charles Darwin discovered that the fourteen species of finch on the Galapagos Islands descended from a single species. This helped him formulate his theory of evolution.

Red-billed Weaver

These African finches breed in colonies up to 10 million nests. They travel in large, locustlike flocks and can cause devastating damage to crops.

Snow Finch

These finches live and breed in the mountainous parts of Asia and Europe where the winters are very cold. Snow finches are one of the very few birds that can survive there.

A Finch's Foot

Leg

Claw

One toe points backward, giving the finch a firm grip on its perch.

Canary

Today's colorful canaries are descended from dull greenish finches that live on the Canary Islands, off the coast of Africa. These birds were first brought to Europe by the Portuguese in the 1400s. Through hundreds of years of selective breeding these popular pets are more colorful than their wild relatives.

FRUIT EATERS

Many birds eat fruits and berries, but some rely more heavily on these foods than others. Such birds are called **frugivores**. Most of them live in tropical regions of the world, where fruits are available throughout the year. Many frugivorous birds can swallow large fruits by opening their beaks very wide.

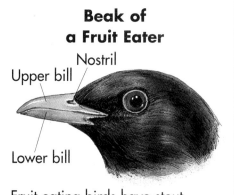

Beak of a Fruit Eater

Nostril

Upper bill

Lower bill

Fruit-eating birds have stout beaks, and can pick berries and larger fruits easily.

Berries
Birds with short beaks peck at fruits and berries, rather than eating them whole.

Toucan
Toucans live in Central and South America. Their colorful beaks are made of porous bone, so they are very light. Their beaks are also very long to help toucans get to fruits that would otherwise be out of reach.

Green Broadbill

The green coloration of this bird helps it remain hidden in its forest home. Its large eyes help it see and find fruit in this dark environment.

Knysna Touraco

Touracos live in Africa, where they feed mainly on fruit. They are often green in color, with bright plumage on the sides of the head. They sometimes have a crest as well.

Perching

The touraco can change the position of one of its toes, to help it to perch.

Orange Dove

Brightly colored fruit doves live on many islands in the Pacific Ocean. The orange dove is found on Fiji.

White-cheeked Cotinga

This bird lives in the Andes Mountains in South America. It feeds entirely on mistletoe berries that grow on the bark of trees.

9

TROPICAL NECTAR FEEDERS

Nectar-feeding birds provide an important service for flowers. As the bird feeds on the nectar it picks up pollen on its beak and feathers. The bird flies to several different flowers, transferring pollen from one flower to another. Once the flowers have been pollinated, they can produce seeds. All nectar-feeding birds are found in the tropical regions of the world where flowers are in bloom year-round.

Chattering Lory

The short-tailed lories, and the lorikeets, which have longer tail feathers, are parrots that feed on nectar and pollen. They live in Australia, Papua New Guinea, and surrounding islands.

Upper beak

Rounded tip

Rough surface of tongue collects pollen

Beak of a Nectar Feeder

Sunbirds

Sunbirds live in parts of Africa and Asia. Cock (male) birds are often brightly colored, and sometimes have **iridescent** plumage, which changes color in sunlight.

Curved bill

Hummingbirds

Hummingbirds have curved or straight bills depending on the type of flower from which they obtain nectar. Hummingbirds live in North, Central, and South America.

Straight bill

Blue-crowned Hanging Parrots

These small parrots can hang upside down to reach flowers. They may also sleep this way, which is why they are sometimes called "bat parrots."

Honeyguide and Ratel

The honeyguide's call attracts the ratel (a badgerlike mammal) to a bee's nest. The ratel breaks the hive open and they take turns eating the honey.

INSECT EATERS

Many birds eat insects and small creatures such as snails and worms. In many parts of the world, birds help control the population of insect pests, like locusts, that destroy crops. When pesticides are used to kill these **invertebrates**, it may also harm the birds that eat them.

Flying, Creeping, Crawling

Some birds catch insects in flight, others dig them up from the ground.

Beak of an Insect Eater

Slender bill probes for insects

Pointed tip

Kiwi

This unusual bird is found only in New Zealand. Unlike most birds who have poor senses of smell, the kiwi uses the nostrils on the end of its upper bill to find food.

Blond-crested Woodpecker
Woodpeckers use their claws to climb trees and hunt for insects. Their tail feathers have firm, pointed ends for extra balance. With their long, sticky, sharp tongues woodpeckers easily pull grubs out from under tree bark.

Oxpecker
Using their strong beaks, these African starlings take ticks off the backs of rhinoceroses and other large animals.

Carmine Bee-eater
Before swallowing its prey, the bee-eater hits the bee against a branch to remove its stinger.

Flamingo
By filtering water through their bills, flamingos catch tiny shrimp and microscopic plants. A special pigment in their food turns their feathers pink. Baby flamingos have straight beaks that curve as they grow older.

13

FISH EATERS

Seabirds are not the only birds that eat fish. A number of other birds prey on fish that live in freshwater lakes, rivers, and ponds. Most fish-eating birds catch fish that they can swallow whole. They may hit the fish against a perch or rock to kill it, and then swallow it headfirst so that it does not become stuck in the bird's throat. The bones and scales may later be spit out as a pellet.

Puffins
The puffin's bill is colorful only during the nesting season. Afterward, this outer part drops off. Puffins rear their chicks in underground burrows. Parents may fly more than twelve miles out to sea to catch fish for their young.

Penguin
Penguins use their wings as flippers to swim underwater. An emperor penguin can dive to a depth of more than 880 feet and can stay underwater for nearly twenty minutes. Besides fish, penguins also feed on squid and shrimp.

Osprey

Found thoughout the United States, ospreys hunt fish in lakes and along coasts. Their keen eyesight enables them to see fish in the water from high above. They dive down and seize the fish with their sharp claws.

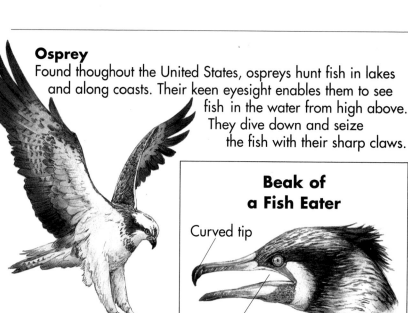

Beak of a Fish Eater

Curved tip

Wide **gape** for swallowing fish whole

Fish eaters have sharp, often saw-edged, bills to grasp their prey.

Kingfisher

Like most waterbirds, the kingfisher's feathers are covered with a waterproofing oil so the bird doesn't get weighed down when it gets wet. Not all species of kingfisher eat fish. Those that hunt insects have much flatter bills than their fish-eating relatives.

Heron

Herons stand still and open their wings to cast a shadow on the water, making it easier to see their prey. Once a fish is within reach, they strike quickly with their daggerlike beaks.

BIRDS OF PREY AND SCAVENGERS

Birds of prey, also called raptors, are the most common meat-eating, or **carnivorous,** group of birds. Some, like hawks, falcons, and eagles, hunt other birds and small animals that they can carry back to their nest easily. Others, such as vultures, are **scavengers**, feeding only on animals that are already dead.

Beak of a Meat Eater

Strong upper beak

Hooked tip

Birds of prey have powerful, broad bills to tear the flesh from an animal's carcass.

Kea
These parrots from the mountains of New Zealand were often blamed for killing sheep and lambs. In fact, they are scavengers and only eat dead animals.

Roadrunner
Skilled at catching lizards and snakes, the roadrunner kills these reptiles with its powerful bill.

Vulture

These huge, scavenging birds of prey glide on hot air currents called thermals. A large crowd of vultures will gather to feed on the carcass of a big animal. Vultures have bald heads. Any feathers would get matted with blood as they fed.

Talons

Powerful foot muscles

Curved claws for a deadly grip

Strong feet and sharp talons help raptors grasp and often kill their prey.

Peregrine Falcon

Diving through the air at speeds of up to 200 miles per hour, peregrines kill their prey by hitting it from above.

Secretary Bird

This unusual long-legged African hawk hunts on the ground, often attacking poisonous snakes. The secretary bird holds the snake down by placing its foot just behind the victim's head. It then batters its prey to death with blows from its wings.

Hand bones

Fingers

Primary flight
feathers

Secondary flight feathers

Nesting

Instead of building a nest out of
twigs and branches, condors
choose a ledge on a cliff face as a
nesting site. This helps keep the
egg away from predators.
The hen lays only one
egg every other year.

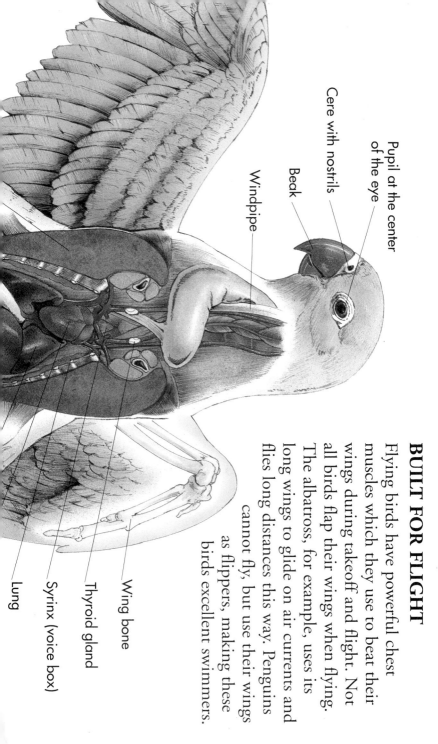

Pupil at the center
of the eye

Cere with nostrils

Beak

Windpipe

Lung

Syrinx (voice box)

Thyroid gland

Wing bone

BUILT FOR FLIGHT

Flying birds have powerful chest muscles which they use to beat their wings during takeoff and flight. Not all birds flap their wings when flying. The albatross, for example, uses its long wings to glide on air currents and flies long distances this way. Penguins cannot fly, but use their wings as flippers, making these birds excellent swimmers.

THE ANDEAN CONDOR: A GIANT IN FLIGHT

These large vultures live in the Andes Mountains of South America. They are the world's heaviest birds of prey. Soaring high above the mountains, they scavenge for food, searching for dead animals, or **carrion**. They sometimes also feed on sick or dying animals. Both male and female have similar black and white feathers,

Radius

Humerus

Ulna

but males are bigger and have a large comblike swelling on top of their heads. Despite their intimidating size, condors are not fierce. In fact, their beaks are so weak that they sometimes have difficulty tearing the flesh off the bones of their prey.

Bare head

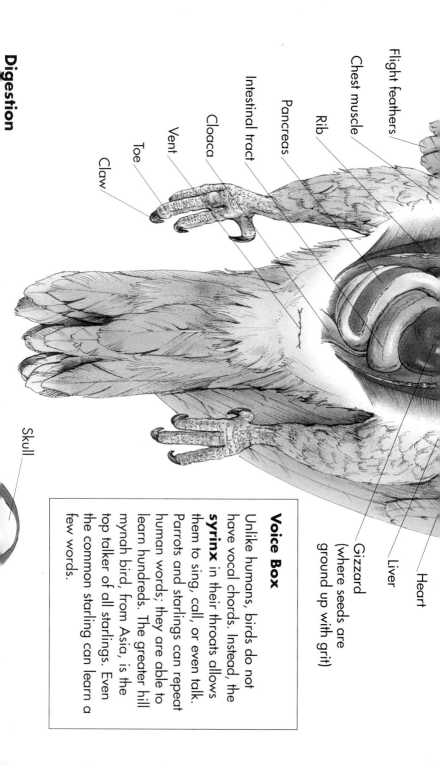

Digestion

Flight feathers

Chest muscle

Rib

Pancreas

Intestinal tract

Cloaca

Vent

Toe

Claw

Gizzard
(where seeds are
ground up with grit)

Liver

Heart

Skull

Voice Box

Unlike humans, birds do not
have vocal chords. Instead, the
syrinx in their throats allows
them to sing, call, or even talk.
Parrots and starlings can repeat
human words; they are able to
learn hundreds. The greater hill
mynah bird, from Asia, is the
top talker of all starlings. Even
the common starling can learn a
few words.

Gliding
Broad wings help these heavy birds glide on warm air currents, called thermals. Condors can soar for hours without having to flap their wings.

Wingspan
The Andean condor has a wingspan of over 10 feet—the widest of any land bird. Only that of the wandering albatross is wider.

21

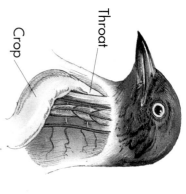

Throat

Crop

Since birds have no teeth, they must swallow their food without chewing it. Food passes from the gullet into the **crop**, where it can be stored. It then moves to the **proventriculus**, where the digestive process begins. Seeds are ground up in the muscular **gizzard**.

Skeletons

A bird's skeleton is strong and light, which is necessary for birds to be able to fly. Its bones are made of hard, porous bone tissue: some are even hollow. The powerful flight muscles are attached to the large breastbone.

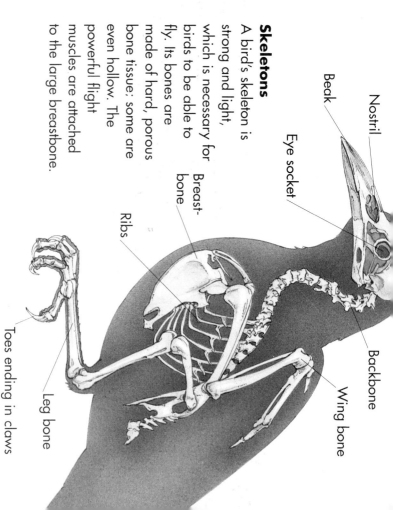

Nostril

Beak

Eye socket

Backbone

Wing bone

Breast-bone

Ribs

Leg bone

Toes ending in claws

EGGS AND HATCHING

All birds lay eggs, but the shape and color varies from species to species. Seabirds which nest on cliffs often lay pear-shaped eggs that won't roll over the edge. Birds that live in open nests lay colorful eggs with markings that blend in with the surroundings. Birds that nest in tree holes or burrows lay white eggs.

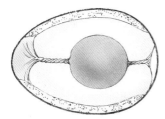

Newly Laid Egg
The yellow yolk at the center provides food for the chick as it develops.

Hatching Egg
The chick cuts its way out of the eggshell using its temporary egg tooth near the tip of its beak.

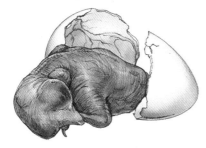

Born Blind
Many chicks are blind and featherless. One or both parents must protect, feed, and keep them warm for two weeks or more, until they are ready to leave the nest.

Eyes Open
Chickens and waterfowl, such as ducks and swans, hatch with their eyes open. They have **down** feathers, and can move around almost immediately. These chicks grow more slowly and stay with their parents longer.

INTERESTING BIRD BEHAVIOR

Birds can be found in all parts of the world and in almost every type of environment, from the icebergs of the Arctic to the tropical forests near the equator. They live in deserts and forests, and on mountains and prairies. Birds have developed many interesting and unique behaviors, adapting to these different habitats in order to survive.

Giant Hummingbird
The largest hummingbird in the world lives in Chile, South America, where the nights can be very cold. To save energy during the cold nights, giant hummingbirds become **torpid** at dusk, appearing dead until the warmth of the sun revives them the next day.

Magpie
Bright, silvery objects—from bottle tops to coins—may be picked up by magpies and hidden, though no one is sure why. In areas where milk is delivered to doorsteps, magpies will steal the shiny foil off the bottles. They will also drink the milk.

Tailorbird
These warblers stitch leaves together to make their nests. They pierce a row of holes in the leaves with their bills, then use the silk of spiders' webs or plant fibers as thread, knotting each stitch individually.

Birds Singing
A bird's song may sound pretty, but it is really a sign of aggression. A bird may sing to warn others out of its territory. Male birds sing to attract females and also to keep away other males.

Poorwill
These unusual birds hibernate through the winter hidden in rock crevices. They build up stores of body fat so that they can survive without feeding.

STARTING A FAMILY

Birds usually breed during the spring and summer months, when the weather is warmer and food is more plentiful. This increases the chances of their chicks' survival. Before two birds mate, the male courts and tries to impress the female. He may change the color of his feathers, perform an elaborate dance, or sing a special song in an effort to grab the female's attention.

Red Bishop
Some birds change color dramatically at the start of the breeding season. Male red bishops' feathers change to a stunning orange and black.

Breeding feathers

Normal feathers

Ruff
Certain birds have display areas, called leks, where males compete for the attention of females. This cock ruff is showing its fine neck plumage to a hen.

Birds' Nests

Ground Nest
Ground nests need to be well hidden to avoid being seen by **predators**.

Hanging Nest
Some birds build basket-shaped nests against the sides of trees or buildings.

Tree Hole
Even here a nest may not be safe. Lizards and snakes may eat eggs and chicks.

Gaping mouth

Feeding
When a parent bird returns to the nest, the chicks open their mouths wide for food. This is called gaping. Their mouths may have markings that show up even in the dark.

Cuckoo
Not all birds hatch their own eggs. The female cuckoo lays her eggs one by one in the nests of other birds. When the cuckoo chick hatches, it pushes the other eggs out of the nest and takes all the food that its foster parents bring. It leaves the nest after about three weeks.

BIRDS ON THE MOVE

Almost half the world's birds regularly fly long distances, or migrate, to and from their breeding grounds each year. In the winter, when the weather is cold and food is scarce, migratory birds fly to warmer climates. Sometimes a sudden shortage of food causes birds to move to places where they are not usually found. These **irruptions** are only temporary; once conditions are better, the birds return to their usual home.

Swallow

Before it was known that swallows migrated from Europe to Africa each fall, it was thought that these birds hibernated at the bottom of ponds. This was because they were seen skimming over the water before they disappeared.

Finding Their Way

Although scientists are not sure exactly how birds know when and where to migrate, they believe birds may use a combination of the Earth's magnetic field and the position of the sun, moon, and stars to find their way. When the days start to get shorter and the weather turns colder, birds know it's time to fly to a warmer climate.

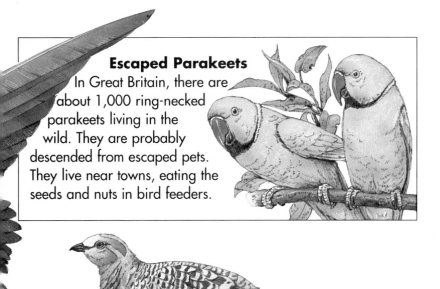

Escaped Parakeets
In Great Britain, there are about 1,000 ring-necked parakeets living in the wild. They are probably descended from escaped pets. They live near towns, eating the seeds and nuts in bird feeders.

Sandgrouse
The sandgrouse, found in southern Europe, Africa, and central Asia, does not usually migrate. However, a large group of sand-grouse may suddenly irrupt and temporarily move to a different area.

Ring-necked Dove
This attractive dove has spread rapidly across Europe from Asia. It is not clear why it extended its range, but these doves can now be seen in many European parks and gardens. Ring-necked doves nest several times during the year in a loose nest of twigs.

31

BIRDS IN DANGER

The greatest threat to birds comes not from their natural predators, but from humans. More than one tenth of the world's birds are endangered because of hunting, pollution, and the destruction of their habitats.

Pesticides

After eating fish and other animals with traces of DDT, a **pesticide,** in their bodies, peregrine falcons began laying soft-shelled eggs that did not hatch. Their numbers decreased dramatically and the birds were in danger of extinction.

Oil Spills

When an oil tanker sinks, the cargo of oil floats on the surface of the sea, smothering the feathers of seabirds. When the birds try to clean their feathers they swallow the oil instead. Many thousands of birds can die as the result of a single oil spill. Cleaning rescued birds takes a long time and is very expensive.

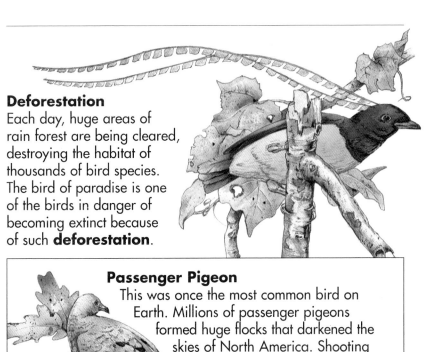

Deforestation

Each day, huge areas of rain forest are being cleared, destroying the habitat of thousands of bird species. The bird of paradise is one of the birds in danger of becoming extinct because of such **deforestation**.

Passenger Pigeon

This was once the most common bird on Earth. Millions of passenger pigeons formed huge flocks that darkened the skies of North America. Shooting and trapping these pigeons for food resulted in their extinction in 1914.

Dodo

The dodo bird lived on the island of Mauritius off the east coast of Africa. It was about the size of a turkey and was unable to fly. By 1680, the dodoes were extinct. They died off because they were overhunted by humans and because pigs brought to Mauritius by Europeans fed on dodo eggs.

SAVING BIRDS

Many organizations are now working to help endangered birds in countries throughout the world. If it is too risky to breed these birds in the wild, they can be bred in safety in **aviaries**. The eggs are hatched in **incubators** and the chicks are reared by hand. The young birds can then eventually be released back to the wild.

St. Lucia Amazon
On the Caribbean island of St. Lucia, a colorful tour bus reminds visitors that the rare Amazon parrots that live there need to be protected.

California Condor
This puppet, which looks like the head of an adult condor, makes the chicks think they are being fed by a real condor. It is important that young birds do not become **imprinted** on the people hand-rearing them.

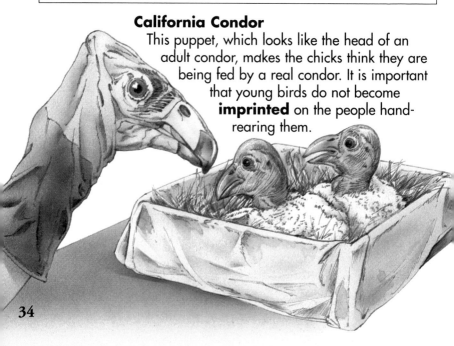

Hawaiian Goose

These geese had nearly become extinct in the wild when a **breeding program** was established to try to save them. Hawaiian geese can now be seen in several zoos. Many have been taken back to Hawaii, where about 800 survive in the wild.

Japanese Crane

In the winter, these cranes migrate from Mongolia to Korea and Japan where they have become a popular tourist attraction. Nearly 1,500 Japanese cranes survive in the wild.

Trumpeter Swan

In 1936 there were only fifteen pairs of these large swans left alive. Conservation efforts have increased their numbers into the thousands.

Feed the Birds

You can help increase the number of birds in your neighborhood by providing food. Peanuts are popular with many birds during the winter. Fill a mesh bag with nuts and hang it in a safe spot where cats and squirrels cannot catch the birds or eat the nuts.

AMAZING BIRD FACTS

- **Night Vision** Owls can spot a mouse from a distance of over 3,000 feet when it is almost completely dark.

- **Fastest Wingbeats** The wings of a hummingbird can beat up to 200 times in a single second. This is so fast that their wing movements appear blurred to our eyes.

- **A Wealthy Bird** The quetzal has not only been adopted as the national symbol of Guatemala, but the country's currency has also been named after this Central American bird.

- **Fast Spread** In just 100 years, starlings have spread across the continent of North America. Today's starlings are descended from a group of 100 birds that were released in New York City's Central Park in the 1890s.

- **Natural Incubators** In southern Australia, mallee fowl do not incubate their eggs like other birds. Instead, they bury them in mounds of soil and rotting vegetation. The heat generated inside the mound allows the chicks to develop. They dig themselves out when they hatch.

- **Standing on an Egg** Ostrich eggs are so strong that they can easily support the weight of a human adult.

- **Tame Talkers** Parrots raised as pets are very talented at mimicking human speech. In the wild, however, they have never been known to mimic.

GLOSSARY

Aviary A place where birds are kept.

Breeding program A plan aimed at producing greater numbers of a bird.

Carnivore An animal that eats meat.

Carrion Dead and decaying flesh.

Crop The enlarged part of a bird's throat where food is stored.

Deforestation The destruction of trees and forests.

Down The soft feathers a bird has when it is born.

Evolution The process by which species change gradually over many years.

Extinct No longer existing.

Flock A large group of birds.

Frugivore An animal that eats fruit.

Gape The width of a bird's open beak.

Gizzard A bird's second stomach where food is ground so that it can be digested.

Imprint The way a young animal recognizes and becomes attached to its mother (or a substitute for her).

Incubator A place where eggs are hatched artificially.

Invertebrate An animal that has no backbone.

Iridescent Showing rainbowlike colors that change in sunlight.

Irruption The sudden appearance or increase of birds in a new area.

Pesticide A chemical used to destroy harmful plants or animals.

Predator An animal that kills and eats other animals.

Proventriculus The front part of a bird's stomach between the crop and gizzard.

Scavenger A bird that eats dead or decaying flesh.

Syrinx A bird's vocal organs.

Torpid Becoming completely still and slowing down body functions to conserve energy.

INDEX *(Entries in **bold** refer to an illustration)*

A
pages

albatross. 21, 24
Andean condor 8-21
archaeopteryx 5

B

beak . . . 5, 6, 8, 10, 12, 13,
. . . . 15, 16, 20, 23, 25
bird of paradise. 33
blond-crested woodpecker13
breeding. 28, 34, 35

C

California condor 34
canary 7
carmine bee-eater 13
chattering lory 10
chick .14, 25, 28, 29, 34, 36
claw 7, 13, 15, 17, 22
Cuban bee hummingbird 5
cuckoo 29

D

Darwin, Charles. 6
digestive process 22
dodo 33

E

egg. 5, 18, 25, 29
. . . . 32, 33, 34, 36
extinct 5, 33, 35

F

finches 6-7
fish-eating birds. 14-15
flamingo 13
fruit-eating birds 8-9

G

gape 15, 29
green broadbill 9

H

Hawaiian goose 35
heron 15
hibernate. 27
hummingbird. . 5, 11, 26, 36

I

insect-eating birds. 12-13

J

Japanese crane **35**

K

kea. 16
kingfisher. 15
kiwi 12
knysna touraco 9

M

magpie. 26
meat-eating birds 16-17
migration 30
moa 5

N

nectar-feeding birds . . . 10-11
nesting. 18, 25, 28-29

O

oil spill 32
orange dove 9
osprey 15
ostrich 5, 36
oxpecker 13